SHARK!

The Truth behind the Terror

by Mike Strong

Reading Consultant:
Timothy Rasinski, Ph.D.
Professor of Reading Education
Kent State University

Content Consultant:
George H. Burgess
Director
International Shark Attack File
Florida Museum of Natural History

Capstone Curriculum Publishing

Capstone Curriculum Publishing materials are published by Capstone Press, P.O. Box 669, 151 Good Counsel Drive, Mankato, Minnesota, 56002
http://www.capstone-curriculum.com
http://www.capstone-press.com

Library of Congress Cataloging-in-Publication Data
Strong, Mike, 1948–
    Shark!: the truth behind the terror/ by Mike Strong.
    p. cm.—(High five reading)
    Includes bibliographical references (p. 46) and index.
    Summary: Explores the facts about sharks and shark attacks, including what these creatures are, how and on what they feed, and how much of a threat they pose to humans.
    ISBN 0-7368-9525-6 (pbk.)—ISBN 0-7368-9547-7 (hardcover)
    1. Sharks—Juvenile literature. 2. Shark attacks—Juvenile literature. [1. Sharks. 2. Shark attacks.] I. Title. II. Series.
QL638.9 .S86 2002
597.3—dc21

                                2002000191

Created by Kent Publishing Services, Inc.
Executive Editor: Robbie Butler
Designed by Signature Design Group, Inc.

Photo Credits:
Cover, pages 4, 24, 25, Jim Watt/Wattstock; page 6, Corbis; pages 8, 12 (bottom), 34, 38, Jeffrey L. Rotman/Corbis; page 11, Corbis; page 15, George Burgess, University of Florida; page 19, Brandon D. Cole/Corbis; pages 17, 18 (top), Stuart Westmoreland/Corbis; page 18, (bottom), James Marshall/Corbis; page 20, Reuters Photo Archive; pages 22, 41 (bottom), Amos Nachoum/Corbis; page 26, Jonathon Bird Photography; page 27, Jeffrey L. Rottman/Corbis; page 37, Christine Osborne/Corbis; page 41(top), Stephen Frink/Corbis

Printed in the United States of America.

1 2 3 4 5 6 08 07 06 05 04 03

Table of Contents

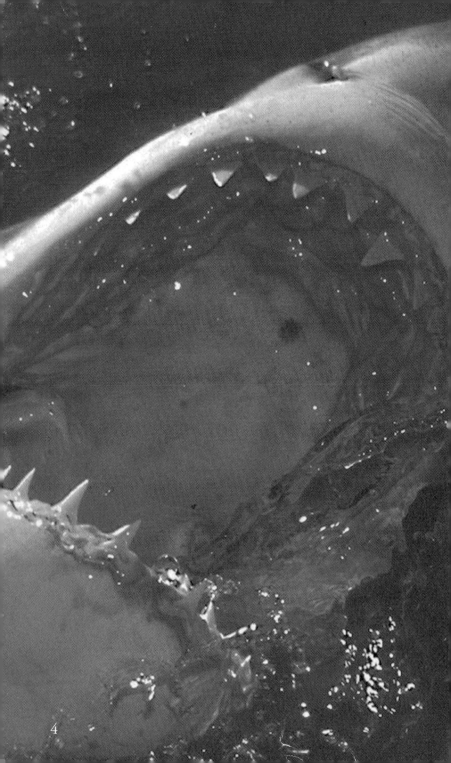

Chapter 1

Help!

You are swimming in the ocean. The day is hot. Your friends are sunbathing back on shore. You see a black fin in the water. It's coming toward you—fast. It's a shark! What do you do?

Surfing in South Africa

Andrew Carter paddled on his surfboard. He was surfing off the coast of South Africa. Suddenly, he felt a huge blow from behind.

Right away, Andrew knew it was a shark. He was **terrified**. The shark **clamped** its huge mouth over Andrew's leg and surfboard. The shark's jaw had to be wider than a doorway. The shark closed its eyes as it sank its teeth deeper into Andrew's leg.

---

terrified: very afraid
clamp: to press down; grip

In the Jaws of Death

The shark began to pull Andrew through the water. It was crushing his leg. He was more than 200 yards (183 meters) from shore, with no help nearby.

A surfer farther away thought the shark was eating Andrew alive. The great white shark appeared to be biting Andrew in half. Terrified, the other surfer headed for shore.

Sharks sometimes attack surfers.

Escape

Then, for some reason, the shark opened its mouth. Andrew thought it was about to take a larger bite. He twisted the board around as the shark let go. Then, he jammed the board into the shark's mouth.

The shark spat the board out. Andrew again clung to the board as the shark swam off. He knew he was losing a lot of blood. A lucky wave carried him back to shore.

Lucky to Be Alive

Two girls on the beach ran to help Andrew. One girl ripped cloth strips from her dress. She stuffed the cloth into Andrew's huge wounds. He felt cold. He could not hear and was losing his sight. He thought he was dying.

But Andrew did not die. It took 2,000 stitches to close his wounds. After many weeks, Andrew's wounds healed.

Nightmare

Bill McNair was fishing with a spear off the coast of California. He was in the water about to spear a fish. Then, he saw a large, gray shape speeding toward him.

Suddenly, two black eyes stared at Bill. He found himself looking at rows of shark teeth. The shark's open mouth zoomed toward him.

Bill threw his spear at the shark. He was on target. The spear stuck in the shark's side. Bill swam back to his boat as fast as he could. He had escaped, but it was a close call. Later, Bill learned that it was a great white shark that had attacked him.

Rodney Fox is a spearfisher, too. A shark also attacked him. Here Rodney holds photos that show the cuts from the shark bite and the stitches that closed them.

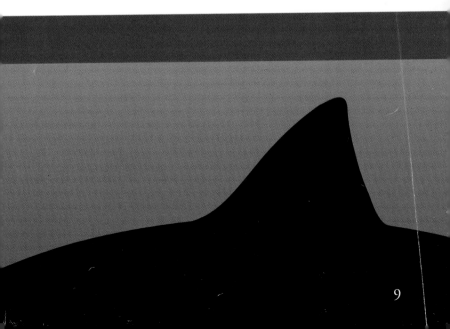

Not So Lucky

A great white shark attacked Henri Bource while he was diving off the coast of Australia. Henri lost a leg from the attack. He was not **bitter**, though. "Sharks do what nature **intended** them to do," he said.

Henri Bource did not quit diving after he was attacked. Here he holds open the mouth of a great white shark.

bitter: upset or angry
intend: to plan

Close Call

Michael Hogan was paddling in his **kayak** off the coast of New Zealand. He heard a loud crunch. Something had bitten through the tough, plastic skin of the kayak. Michael was tossed into the water.

Imagine a shark biting this kayak.

A great white shark held the kayak in its mouth. But the shark let it go and swam away. Michael escaped unhurt.

The Truth, but Not the Whole Truth

These stories are true. Sharks are **predators**. They sometimes attack people. But sharks don't attack people very often.

It's a good thing, too. Sharks are very good predators. In the next chapter, you will find out why.

---

kayak: a covered, narrow boat
predator: an animal that hunts other animals for food

11

Grey reef shark

Nurse shark

Hammerhead shark

CHAPTER 2

What Is a Shark?

*Sharks both frighten and **fascinate** people. It has long been that way. Some people once **worshipped** sharks. Why do you think people find sharks so interesting?*

Older than the Dinosaurs

Sharks have been around for nearly 400 million years. Dinosaurs didn't show up until 245 million years ago. The dinosaurs died out. But sharks just keep living!

In the ocean, the shark is a top predator. And nothing hunts sharks except other, bigger sharks—and people.

---

fascinate: to have great appeal or interest
worship: to treat like a god

No Bones about Them

Most sharks have no bones. Their **skeletons** are made of **cartilage**. The cartilage is hard like bone, but it is also **flexible**.

The jaws of most sharks connect loosely with their skulls. These sharks can open their mouths very wide. That makes it easy to bite large **prey**.

Keep Moving or Drown

Some sharks must move forward to breathe and stay afloat. Water flows over the shark's **gills** as it swims. The gills take in oxygen from the water. Then the water flows out through gill slits. These openings are on the sides of the shark's head. Big sharks have five to seven pairs of gill slits.

---

skeleton: the bones that support and protect the body
cartilage: tough, bendy material that makes up the skeleton of the shark
flexible: easy to bend
prey: an animal that is being hunted
gill: in sharks or other fish, an organ that takes in oxygen

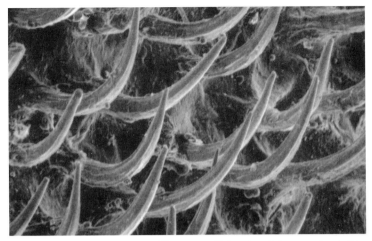

Close-up of the denticles on sharkskin

Rough Stuff

Sharkskin is covered with **scales** called *denticles*. The scales are very hard. People once used dried sharkskin as sandpaper.

Brainier than You Think

Sharks are pretty smart. They can remember things as well as white rats or pigeons. In tests, sharks found their way through a **maze** as fast as rabbits.

---

scale: one of the small pieces of hard skin that cover the body of a fish
maze: a puzzle made with a series of paths

They Can Sense You

Sharks can feel small changes and movements in the water. Under the shark's skin, tubes with fine hairs sense almost any motion. This helps sharks find prey.

Around their **snouts**, sharks have groups of cells called *electro-receptors*. These cells help them **detect** signals put out by prey.

They Can Hear and Smell You, Too

A shark hears through a small **duct** inside its head. A shark can hear well enough to detect a fish struggling far away. Sharks also have a strong sense of smell. They can smell a single drop of blood in a million drops of water.

---

snout: the mouth and usually the nose of an animal
detect: to notice or find something
duct: a tube in the body where air or liquid flows

Going in Blind

A great white shark has good eyesight.
But it attacks blind. At the last second, thin
layers of skin move across the shark's eyes to
protect them in an attack. Then the shark
uses its other senses to guide it.

Speed Freaks

Blue and mako sharks can swim at more
than 30 miles (48 kilometers) per hour
for short stretches. They can attack at
fast speeds.

Great white shark

Big Biters

Sharks have rows of teeth. When a tooth breaks off, it is replaced. Another tooth moves forward from the inside of the jaw to take its place.

Each type of shark has its own kind of teeth. The tiger shark and the great white shark have teeth with **jagged** edges. These edges help these sharks tear the flesh of large fish. Sharp, spiky teeth help the mako shark spear small fish and squid. The large basking shark does not need large teeth. It only feeds on tiny sea creatures like **plankton**.

In the top photo, you can see the large teeth of a great white shark. In the bottom photo, you can see the small teeth of a swell shark.

jagged: uneven and sharp
plankton: tiny creatures that drift or float in the sea

Born to Hunt

Most sharks give birth to live young. Others lay eggs. In both cases, the baby shark, called a *pup*, has to feed itself. The pup must learn how to find food by itself. It also must learn how to stay away from predators.

What Do You Think?

Now you have some idea what makes sharks such awesome predators. Can you see why they have **survived** for so long? What do you think is a shark's best **weapon**?

A baby horn shark

survive: to continue to live
weapon: a tool used in an attack

A sand tiger shark lunches on a reef shark.

CHAPTER 3

What's for Lunch?

Where do sharks live? How do sharks find prey?
How often do they eat? Do all sharks eat the same
food? What questions do you have about sharks?

Sharks Everywhere!

Sharks live all over the world. They can be
found in **tropical** waters and cold Arctic
seas. Some even live in freshwater rivers.

All sharks are **carnivores** (KAR-nuh-vors).
That means they hunt and eat meat. Most
sharks need to eat a large meal every two to
three days. Some sharks can go for weeks
without eating, though. These sharks slowly
use up food stored in their bodies.

---

tropical: found in the hot area of Earth near the equator
carnivore: something that eats meat

Looking for Food

Many large sharks follow their prey as it **migrates**. Others, like the great white shark, travel to waters where their prey lives. Tiger, hammerhead, and bull sharks often hunt near **reefs**. These reefs provide sharks with plenty of food.

The fastest shark, the mako, chases schools of tuna. The mako shark uses its long, sharp teeth to spear the tuna. Then it swallows the fish whole. The tiger and the great white shark look for large prey. These include porpoises, seals, and turtles.

Mako shark

migrate: to move from one region to another
reef: strips of rock, sand, and coral near the surface of the ocean

It's No Use Hiding

Hammerhead sharks use their electro-receptors to find prey. They can find a stingray buried in the sand. Hammerheads can eat an entire stingray—complete with the ray's powerful stinger!

The angel shark hides in sand on the ocean floor. It waits for prey to come by. Then it quickly attacks by surprise.

Bite-size Chunks

The small cookie-cutter shark has large, razor-sharp teeth. It bites chunks from the undersides of whales and dolphins. Sometimes, the cookie-cutter shark even attacks submarines! Maybe it thinks they are whales.

Feeding Frenzy

Sometimes humans make sharks act wild.
If fishing boats dump large amounts of dead
fish and blood into the water, sharks may
go into a feeding **frenzy**. They swim around
fast, biting at anything that gets close. This
includes other sharks.

As blood flows, sharks become even more
wild. The food may be gone, but the sharks
keep biting chunks out of each other.

Sharks in a feeding frenzy

---

frenzy: wild activity

Attack from Below

The great white shark attacks with speed. It charges from below and behind its prey. To attack a seal, a great white shark will take a big bite from the seal. Then it will wait for the seal to bleed to death.

After the seal is dead, the shark bites off large hunks of flesh and **blubber**. It carries the hunks into deeper water, where it eats them whole.

A great white shark opens wide.

blubber: the fat under the skin of a whale or seal

Mixed Krill

The basking shark isn't a big biter. It feeds on tiny plankton, **krill**, and **larvae**. It swims slowly with its huge mouth open. Like a giant vacuum cleaner, it takes in water with small fish and krill.

Basking shark

krill: small, shrimp-like creatures
larvae: the young of tiny sea creatures

Tiger shark

Inside a Tiger Shark

People have found some very strange things inside the stomachs of tiger sharks. These include a raincoat, deer antler, rubber tire, chicken coop, and a driver's license.

Food for Thought

So what about people? Do you think people are part of a shark's meal plan? Read on and find out.

Sharks that Attack Humans

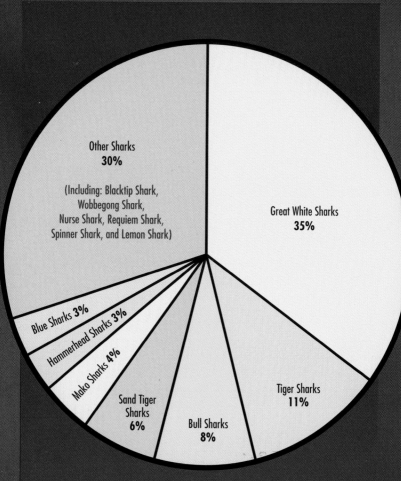

Other Sharks
30%

(Including: Blacktip Shark,
Wobbegong Shark,
Nurse Shark, Requiem Shark,
Spinner Shark, and Lemon Shark)

Great White Sharks
35%

Blue Sharks **3%**

Hammerhead Sharks **3%**

Mako Sharks **4%**

Sand Tiger
Sharks
6%

Bull Sharks
8%

Tiger Sharks
11%

*Sharks don't normally attack people. But it can happen.
This is a pie chart of 100 shark attacks against humans.
The chart shows the average number of known attacks
by each type of shark.*

CHAPTER 4

Sharks and People

*What's the real story behind shark attacks? Are sharks usually **dangerous**? When is it safe to swim? What can you do to be safe?*

How Dangerous Are Sharks?

Sharks don't normally attack people. In fact, you are more likely to be killed by a falling coconut than attacked by a shark! Thousands more people drown each year than suffer shark attacks.

In an average year, sharks kill only 10 people and injure up to 100. Millions of people swim in the ocean every year. So that is not many shark attacks. Still, it makes sense to keep out of a shark's way.

---

dangerous: likely to cause harm or injury

Why Sharks Attack

Sharks don't go looking for a fight. But sometimes a shark will attack a human. Usually, it does this because it thinks the human is prey.

Looking for Food

Sharks often gather near beaches to look for food. When the **surf** crashes or the water is **murky**, sharks may make mistakes. Moving arms and legs may make humans look like fish, a shark's prey. The shark will grab at a leg or a foot, then take off. **Usually**, no harm results.

Sharks sometimes attack surfers. From below the water, a surfer may look like a seal or turtle to a shark. The shark may think the surfer is dinner and attack.

---

surf: waves that break on the shore or a reef
murky: dark or cloudy
usually: normally or commonly

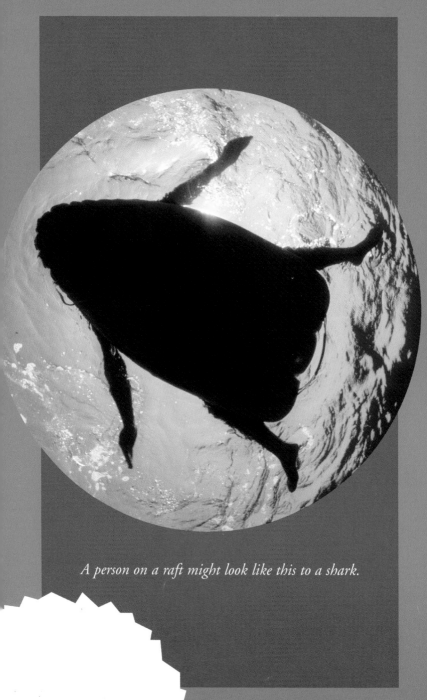

A person on a raft might look like this to a shark.

Bump-and-Bite Attacks

Some attacks happen in deeper waters. Again, the shark probably thinks the person is prey. The shark may charge and bite. If the shark keeps biting, the victim may be hurt or even killed.

In a bump-and-bite attack, the shark first bumps the victim. The shark is testing. It wants to see whether the prey is okay to eat. Then the shark will attack. Bump-and-bite attacks also can lead to injury or death.

Risky Places

Most attacks take place off the coasts of Australia, North America (mainly Florida), South Africa, and Hawaii. People like to swim in warm water. Many types of sharks like to do this as well.

Safety First

A shark attack is less likely to happen if you follow the following safety tips. If you do see a shark, stay calm. Remember, the shark is just as afraid as you are.

Shark Safety Tips

Do not enter the water alone.
Go with a buddy or group of friends.

Sharks often feed at **dusk** and **dawn**.
Do not enter the water at these times.

Avoid murky water.

Do not splash a lot.

If you see a shark, swim quickly, but without splashing, toward the shore.

Sharks can sense blood from a long way off.
Keep out of the water if you are bleeding.

Don't wear shiny swimwear, jewelry, or watches.
Sharks sometimes attack shiny objects.

Never tease a shark by pulling
its tail or poking it.

dusk: the time of day after sunset when it is nearly dark
dawn: the beginning of a day; sunrise

Fishers pull in a sandbar shark.

CHAPTER 5

Sharks under Attack

Are you still afraid of sharks? Do you think sharks are afraid of us? They should be. People kill millions of sharks each year. Sharks need us to protect them.

People Attack!

Humans kill about 20 to 30 million sharks a year. Some people think this is too many. These people are trying to find ways to protect sharks. One way is to limit how many sharks fishers may catch.

Why are these people worried about catching too many sharks? Sharks don't produce as many young as most fish do. When we kill sharks, the shark **population** gets smaller. As it gets smaller, fewer shark pups are born as well.

---

population: the total number of a living thing

Pollution

Sharks face other threats. For example, **pollution** hurts sharks. People may pollute the sea with oil or other harmful matter. Other sea creatures may take in this pollution. Sharks eat some of these creatures. This often poisons the sharks.

Shark Fin Soup

Some restaurants serve shark fin soup. In 1998, fishers caught 60,000 sharks off the coast of Hawaii. They caught them simply for their fins. They dumped the rest of the shark's body into the sea. The United States does not allow this anymore. It is trying to get other countries to stop this as well.

---

pollution: harmful matter that damages water, air, or soil

Shark fins hang to dry in the sun.

What Else Comes from Sharks?

People eat sharks for food. But people make other products from dead sharks as well. These products include liver oil for vitamins and medicines. Sharks' teeth are used for jewelry.

*Pills made from
shark liver oil*

Shark steaks

Sharks Need Friends!

Without our help, the shark population will keep falling. Several countries now **protect** the great white shark. Whale, basking, and sand tiger sharks are also protected in some areas of the world.

So Much We Don't Know

We need to learn more about sharks. With more study, we can better protect sharks in the future.

Humans and sharks can live in greater **harmony**. With our help, there will be sharks to fascinate and frighten us for many years to come.

---

protect: to keep safe
harmony: peace

Shark Album

Great White Shark
Habitat—near shores in **temperate** areas
Size—averages 12–16 feet (3.7–4.9 meters); heaviest—7,000 pounds (3,175 kilograms)
Color—gray to blue-gray top; white bottom
Teeth—**triangular** and saw-like
Diet—turtles, fish, rays, other sharks, seals, sea lions, dead whales
Danger to humans—high

Tiger Shark
Habitat—tropical waters worldwide
Size—averages around 10 feet (3 meters)
Color—gray-brown top; off-white bottom
Teeth—saw-like, razor sharp, and curved
Diet—fish, turtles, crabs, mammals, sea birds, and other sharks
Danger to humans—high

habitat: the place where an animal naturally lives
temperate: not very hot or very cold
triangular: shaped like a triangle, with three corners

Mako Shark

Habitat—warm and cool waters

Size—averages 6–10 feet (1.8–3.0 meters)

Color—gray-blue top; white bottom

Teeth—long, thin, and sharp; useful for spearing slippery fish

Diet—schools of fish, such as tuna, herring, mackerel, and swordfish

Danger to humans—medium

Bull Shark

Habitat—tropical and subtropical oceans; also found close to shore, including rivers and **estuaries**

Size—averages 7 feet (2 meters)

Color—gray top, off-white bottom

Teeth—triangular, saw-like, and very sharp

Diet—fish, turtles, birds, mollusks, crustaceans, and dolphins

Danger to humans—high

---

estuary: the wide part of a river where it joins the sea

Epilogue

Strange but True Shark Facts

- The great white shark's bite is more than twice as strong as a lion's.

- Mako sharks can leap above the water like dolphins.

- Bull sharks have been found 1,700 miles (2,736 kilometers) up the Mississippi River and 2,500 miles (4,023 kilometers) up the Amazon River.

- The megamouth shark was discovered in 1976. The discovery was a surprise because it is the third largest shark.

- Sharks are cleaned by small fish and shrimps. These creatures remove **parasites** from sharkskin.

parasite: an animal or plant that gets food by living on or inside another animal or plant

- A large great white shark eats up to 11 tons (9.98 metric tons) of meat a year.

- The great white shark can hold its head out of the water. It can see what is happening on the surface.

- The spotted wobbegong shark's skin looks just like a coral reef.

- About 80 percent of all shark **species** have never been known to attack humans.

- Sharks often follow fishing boats. They hope to catch a free meal. Sharks eat fish that are thrown back in the sea.

- Many deep-water sharks are **luminous**. They have light organs in their bodies.

species: groups of animals or plants
luminous: shining or glowing

Glossary

bitter: upset or angry

blubber: the fat under the skin of a whale or seal

carnivore: something that eats meat

cartilage: tough, bendy material that makes up the skeleton of the shark

clamp: to press down; grip

dangerous: likely to cause harm or injury

dawn: the beginning of a day; sunrise

detect: to notice or find something

duct: a tube in the body where air or liquid flows

dusk: the time of day after sunset when it is nearly dark

estuary: the wide part of a river where it joins the sea

fascinate: to have great appeal or interest

flexible: easy to bend

frenzy: wild activity

gill: in sharks or other fish, an organ that takes in oxygen

habitat: the place where an animal naturally lives

harmony: peace

intend: to plan

jagged: uneven and sharp

kayak: a covered, narrow boat

krill: small, shrimp-like creatures

larvae: the young of tiny sea creatures

luminous: shining or glowing

maze: a puzzle made with a series of paths

migrate: to move from one region to another

murky: dark or cloudy

parasite: an animal or plant that gets food by living on or inside another animal or plant

plankton: tiny creatures that drift or float in the sea

pollution: harmful matter that damages water, air, or soil

population: the total number of a living thing

predator: an animal that hunts other animals for food

prey: an animal that is being hunted

protect: to keep safe

reef: strips of rock, sand, and coral near the surface of the ocean

scale: one of the small pieces of hard skin that cover the body of a fish

skeleton: the bones that support and protect the body

snout: the mouth and usually the nose of an animal

species: groups of animals or plants

surf: waves that break on the shore or a reef

survive: to continue to live

temperate: not very hot or very cold

terrified: very afraid

triangular: shaped like a triangle, with three corners

tropical: found in the hot area of Earth near the equator

usually: normally or commonly

weapon: a tool used in an attack

worship: to treat like a god

Bibliography

Deady, Kathleen W. *Great White Sharks.*
Predators in the Wild. Mankato, Minn.:
Capstone Press, 2001.

MacQuitty, Miranda. *Shark.* Eyewitness Books.
New York: DK Publishing, 2000.

Schaefer, Lola M. *Sharks: Hunters of the Deep.*
The Wild World of Animals. Mankato, Minn.:
Capstone Press, 2001.

Stonehouse, Bernard. *A Visual Introduction to
Sharks, Skates and Rays.* Animal Watch. New York:
Checkmark Books, 1999.

Useful Addresses

Florida Museum of Natural History
International Shark Attack File
University of Florida
P.O. Box 117800
Gainesville, FL 32611–2710

The Shark Trust
National Marine Aquarium
The Rope Walk
Coxside, Plymouth PL4 OLF
United Kingdom

Steinhart Aquarium
California Academy of Sciences
55 Concourse Drive
Golden Gate Park
San Francisco, CA 94118–4599

Internet Sites

California Academy of Sciences
www.calacademy.org/

The International Shark Attack File
www.flmnh.ufl.edu/fish/Sharks/ISAF/ISAF.htm

Zoom Sharks: All about Sharks!
www.EnchantedLearning.com/subjects/sharks

Index